Kimo[illegible]

きもの

日本語 Level 2

Workbook

Suzanne Burnham
and Yukiko Saegusa

Illustrated by Alex Jankovic

CIS Educational

CIS Educational
245 Cardigan Street
Carlton Victoria Australia 3053
Telephone (03) 347 9144
Facsimile (03) 347 0175

First published as a book in 1991 (twice)
Reprinted 1993

Edited by Curtis Watson
Designed by Josie Semmler
Illustrated by Alex Jankovic
Additional illustrations by Bill Farr and Josie Semmler
Crane character by Randy Glusac
Typeset by Josie Semmler on Apple Macintosh

Printed in Australia by Griffin Paperbacks

ISBN 0 949919 82 9

Contents・もくじ

Introduction・はじめに

The exercises and activities in the *Kimono Level 2 Workbook* are based on the language and cultural information presented in the corresponding units of the *Kimono Level 2 Textbook.*

Each unit in the *Workbook* comprises the following elements:

ききましょう

This section contains listening comprehension exercises which are performed on the *Kimono Cassettes.*

れんしゅうしましょう

These are written exercises which reinforce the material treated orally in each unit. They come in a variety of forms and form the bulk of the material in the *Workbook.*

まんがについて

In this section there are reading comprehension exercises based on the cartoon story. Multiple choice, true or false and answer in日本語 types of exercises are included.

タスク

These activities require students to attempt to put language acquired in the unit to real communicative use. In some cases no space has been left for students to write. They are therefore free to write as much as they like, present their work in an interesting format and illustrate it as well.

日本について

Exercises and activities in this section exploit the cultural material contained in each せいかつ Unit.

Script

Kimono Level 2 introduces katakana in a separate section of the *Workbook.* Katakana is presented in four sets (including drinks, fruit and vegetables, names of countries) and recognition of these words is seen as the initial activity prior to writing. Katakana is introduced into the text and workbook exercises from Unit 3. It can, however, be commenced immediately and learnt concurrently with Units 1 and 2. Sixteen kanji are introduced and have been selected for their frequency of use.

漢字とカタカナ

New kanji are presented with stroke order, readings and practice squares.

れんしゅう

These exercises enable practice of the new kanji and reinforcement of katakana.

第一課・おみやげ です。どうぞ。

ききましょう

A あきこさん does *earobikusu* wherever she can. Listen as she explains where she exercises every day. Write the かんじ number in the box below the illustration.

B Listen to these people deciding where to eat. For each dialogue, write the number in the box above the picture to indicate where they will go to eat.

C These people are being interviewed about their weekend and spare-time activities. Write the appropriate かんじ number in the box below the illustration which represents the activity.

D Listen as these four students introduce themselves to you. For each student use a different coloured pen to highlight the following:

1 where they live
2 what year level they are at school
3 what they like to do in their spare time

Name	City	School level	Interests
まえだ ようこ	Yokohama	2nd year junior high school	Playing computer games
さかきばら ひろし	Osaka	1st year senior high school	Playing guitar
せきね かなえ	Sapporo	4th year primary school	Playing soccer
みずの そういち	Kobe	1st year primary school	Reading
	Tokyo	3rd year junior high school	Playing with the cat

れんしゅう しましょう

A Write a sentence saying what each きもの character did yesterday and where they did it.

例:

1 Hose くん は うち で terebi を みました。

2 ______________________________

3 ______________________________

4 ______________________________

5 ______________________________

6 ______________________________

7 ______________________________

B Imagine you are going to send this school photo of you and your brothers and sisters to your pen-pal in Japan. Write details in 日本語 of their ages and school levels in the spaces below.

____

____

____

____

____

C Your Japanese friend has said the following things to you. Choose an appropriate response from the expressions given.

いいえ、そうでも ないです。
いいえ。
どうも ありがとう。
そう ですね。

1 おみやげ です。どうぞ。 ____________________

2 Piano が じょうず ですね。 ____________________

3 おそく なって すみません。 ____________________

4 いい おてんき ですね。 ____________________

5 日本語 が じょうず ですね。 ____________________

D You are going to visit the students on page 八 of your textbook. Which of the following おみやげ will you give to them? Write the student's name on a gift tag.

あたらしい Eruton Jon の kassetto
やきゅう の ooru-sutaa の posutaa
rokku konsaato の chiketto
いぬ の 本

E Krista is one of those people who talks a lot and jumps from one subject to another. She's actually telling you about herself here but has got side-tracked! Write what Krista has said.

1 In my spare time, I listen to CDs in my room.

____

2 I'm good at aerobics. I go to the gym on the weekend.

____

3 What an interesting watch! Where did you buy it?

____

4 My little brother is in first year at primary school. Yesterday he did homework. He's so cute!

____

____

5 Let's meet over there at 1.30.

____

6 I'll introduce you to my new friend. He's really cool!

____

F Pazuru

どこ で たいいく を しますか。

							し	ま	す	。

To work out what is missing, find the place words for the illustrations in the puzzle (horizontally and vertically). Seven letters will remain to spell out the answer.

こ	く	う	こ	う	た
う	こ	と	い	に	わ
て	う	し	い	こ	く
い	こ	ょ	う	う	へ
か	う	か	み	え	や
ま	ち	ん	ん	ん	で

Tasuku

Answer the five questions below, and you will have prepared a short じこしょうかい. Write it out in the space below.

1 おなまえは なん ですか。
2 どこ に すんで いますか。
3 なんさい ですか。
4 なんねんせい ですか。
5 ひまなときなに を しますか。

Don't be too modest ー say what you are good at as well!

Now that you have prepared your じこしょうかい, why not try the suggestions below.

- Get together with a group of your friends and tape it. The cassettes could be exchanged with another school using きもの, or a school in Japan. Perhaps せんせい would like to have them to get to know you better.
- Video it. A video is fun to exchange with another school!
- Make じこしょうかい posters.
- Present it to another class studying 日本語. Perhaps you could supplement your talk with some or all of the resources you may have produced for the activities above.

日本について

A In her letter, Simone referred to old Mr Tanaka's irritation with がいらいご (borrowed words). There are many がいらいご used in 日本語. Some people use them to appear 'modern' and sometimes they are used to describe the Western version of the item. Below is a list of がいらいご and a list of Japanese words. Try to match the two lists. (Some pairs you already know.) To find out the meanings of the Japanese words that you do not know, you will need a Japanese-English dictionary.

chiketto	しゅうまつ
terehon	おとうさん
sutoroberii	くつした
cherii	くだもの
miruku	けっこんしき
pen keesu	しゃしんき
koohii shoppu	ももいろ
sokkusu	さくらんぼ
uiikuendo	ぎゅうにゅう
papa	ふでばこ
kamera	いちご
furuutsu	きっぷ
pinku	おかあさん
uedingu	きっさてん
sukuuru	なまえ
mama	でんわ
neemu	がっこう

B おみやげ

List some おみやげ that are popular with Japanese tourists visiting your country.

C A friend of your family recently spent a few days in 日本. He now tells everyone all about what he saw. This friend doesn't worry too much about facts and he really doesn't know as much as he thinks he does. Below is some of the information he is spreading around. After reading Simone's letter, see if you can fix up his misapprehensions.

・Most things in Japan are organized and run by young people.

・*Pachinko* is a very popular game with all ages and people win lots of money.

・Japanese has so much English in it, that within a few years everyone will speak and write in English.

・A good, useful souvenir to bring back from Japan is a telephone card.

かんじ 漢字

日	本	月
Meaning: *sun, day*	Meaning: *origin, book*	Meaning: *moon, month*
Readings ひ (び) にち (に)	Readings ほん (ぽん, ぼん)	Readings がつ、げつ
日本 (にほん) 日よう日 (にちようび)	日本 (にほん) 本 (ほん)	一月 (いちがつ) 四月 (しがつ) 月よう日(げつようび)

日 日 日 日 日

日 日

本 本 本 本 本 本

本 本

月 月 月 月 月

月 月

れんしゅう

A Label these pictures.

[ ][ ]
にほん

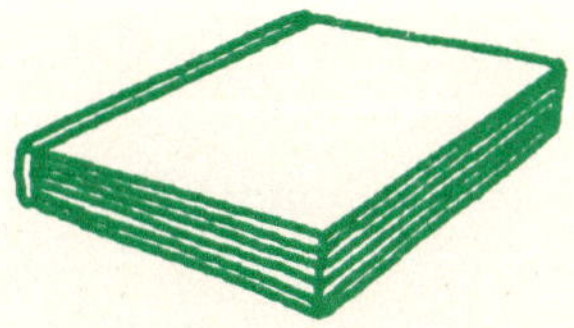

[ ]
ほん

[ ][ ][語][の][ ]
にほん　ほん

[ ][ ]
さんがつ

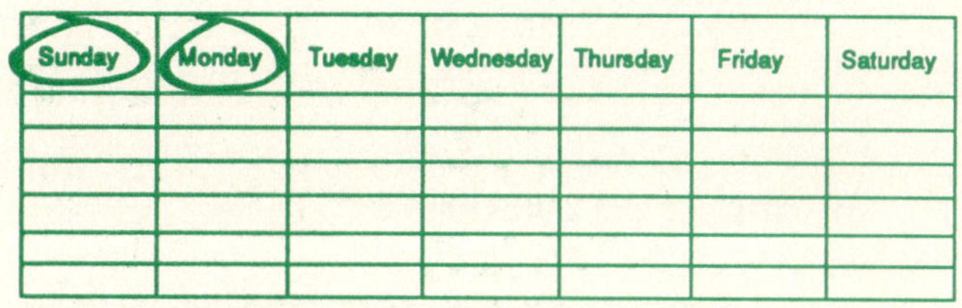

[ ][よ][う][ ]
にち　び

[ ][よ][う][ ]
げつ　び

B Rewrite these sentences changing the underlined words to かんじ.

なつやすみに にほん に いきました。にほん で おもしろい ほん を かいました。

____

にちようび の しちじ はん に にほん の えいが を みましょう。

____

C Complete this sentence using かんじ for the month.

たんじょうび は [ ][ ][ ] です。

まんが に ついて

A Read the まんが in 第一課 of your textbook and then decide whether the following statements are true or false. Write はい if the statement is true and いいえ if it is false.

1 Jianguくん は やすみ に Hawai に いきました。 ________

2 Teriiくん は あたらしい ともだち です。 ________

3 Maikuくん は やきゅう の chanpion です。 ________

4 はなこさん は ひまなとき supootsu を します。 ________

5 ゆうこさん は とうきょう dizuniirando で おみやげ を かいました。 ________

6 Maikuくん の おみやげ は おおきい T-shatsu です。 ________

B Answer the questions in 日本語.

1 あたらしい ともだち は だれ ですか。

____

2 Amandaさん は やすみ に なに を しましたか。

____

3 Maikuくん は なんさい ですか。

____

4 はなこさん は なんねんせい ですか。

____

5 はなこさん と ゆうこさん は 日本 で なに を かいましたか。

____

C Write down, in えい語, three things that you learnt about Maikuくん from his じこしょうかい and three things that はなこさん told you about herself in her じこしょうかい.

第二課・Maikuくん は どこ?

ききましょう

A The きもの characters are all busy. Draw a line connecting the character to the activity.

B Listen to these people describing their dogs. Draw a line connecting the dog to its name.

C Listen as ひでたか invites different friends out. Decide whether his friends accept the invitation or are unable to go because of the time or activity suggested. Highlight or circle the response of each friend.

	Accept	Activity unsuitable	Time unsuitable
	Accept	Activity unsuitable	Time unsuitable
	Accept	Activity unsuitable	Time unsuitable
	Accept	Activity unsuitable	Time unsuitable
	Accept	Activity unsuitable	Time unsuitable

れんしゅう しましょう

A This illustration shows various parts of the body. Find the characters' features and complete the list. The first has been done for you.

1 ゆうこさん の かお。

2 Amandaさん の ____________________

3 Jianguくん の ____________________

4 Teriiくん の ____________________

5 Maikuくん の ____________________

6 はなこさんの ____________________

7 せんせい の ____________________

8 Hoseくん の ____________________

9 Chappii の ____________________

B What are these people doing? For each drawing, write a caption explaining what the person is doing.

____

____

____

____

____

____

____

____

____

____

____

____

____

____

C Complete this table with the て form of each verb. (You have not yet learnt some of these verbs but, using the patterns for the て form, you will be able to give the て form of these verbs too.)

Weak		Irregular	
たべます		いきます	
しめます		きます	
おきます (get up)		します	
ねます (go to bed)			
Strong			
すわります		かきます	
かえります (return)		ひきます	
つくります (make)		はきます (wear)	
かいます		あそびます	
つかいます (use)		のみます	
たちます		よみます	
まちます		かします	
		はなします (speak)	

D You probably have strong views about who is good-looking or pretty, or what is strange or quiet... Give your opinion by completing these statements.

1 ______________________________ は ゆうめいな ひと です。

2 ______________________________ は hansamu ですね。

3 ______________________________ は とても きれいですよ。

4 ______________________________ は しずかですね。

5 ______________________________ は いや です。

E Teriiくん has not yet worked out the difference between い and な adjectives. He has therefore left blanks in his homework. Help him out by adding な when it is necessary.

1 すてき □ おみやげです。
2 おいしい □ keekiです。
3 かわいい □ ねこです。
4 いや □ しゅくだいです。
5 きれい □ せんせいです。
6 むずかしい □ かんじです。
7 へん □ ひと です。
8 ゆうめい □ tenisuの せんしゅ です。
9 しずか □ こうえんです。
10 おもしろい □ 本 です。

F Pazuru

Your friends have all had a guess at the answer to the question,

けいこさんは いま なにを していますか.

Write all ten guesses (in日本語) in the grid below and then, to find the correct answer, transfer the circled characters to the boxes below the grid.

1 She is washing her face.
2 She is studying geography.
3 She is looking at photos.
4 She is playing the piano.
5 She is drinking cola.
6 She is reading the paper.
7 She is waiting for the train.
8 She is listening to music.
9 She is drawing a picture.
10 She is buying souvenirs.

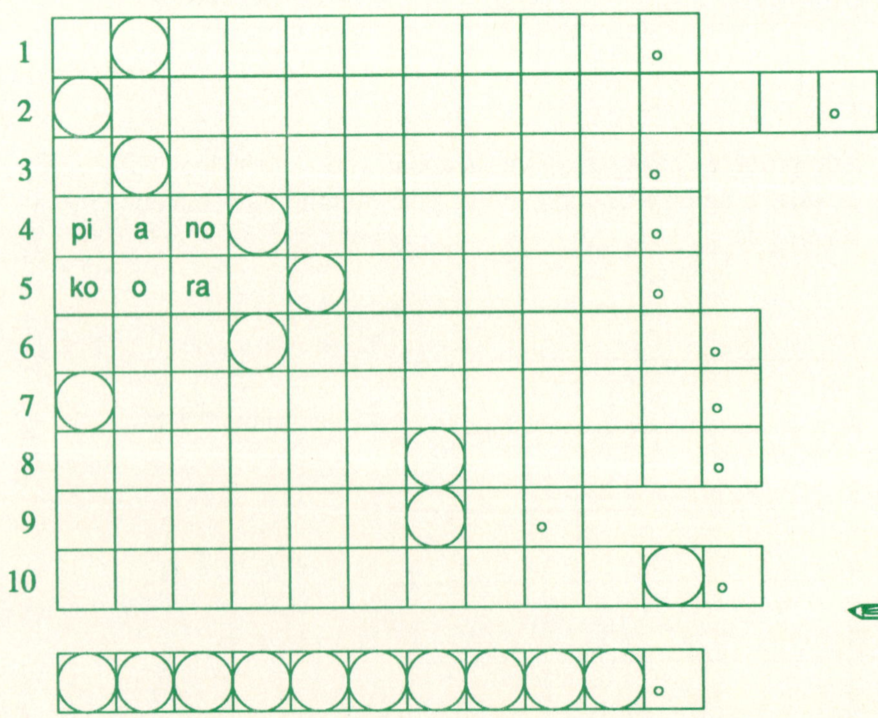

G Below are the photo and part of the letter your friend, Jamie, received from his pen friend, こうじくん. こうじくん did not write the names of the people in the photo on the back of it and so Jamie doesn't know which person is こうじくん. Read the letter, name the people in the photo and work out which person is こうじくん.

Jeimii くんへ

こんにちは。おげんきですか。ぼくは げんき です。
きょう は *kurasu* の ともだち の しゃしん を みて
ください。よしこさんは めが おおきい です。
いさむくんは あしが ながい です。*Basuketto booru* の
せんしゅ です。ゆうたくんと まゆみさんは みみ が
おおきい です。まさひこくんは かみ の け が ながい
です。みかさんはせがたかいです。

Tasuku

Design an invitation for a birthday party, outing or activity. You will need to write what time the party is and, of course, where it will be. If you are planning an invitation to an outing or activity, state where and at what time you will be meeting. Remember to give your address and phone number for replies!

日本 に ついて

Simone, in her 日本語 letter on page 二十三 of your textbook, used many Japanese letter-writing customs. From her letter, write down the following:

- how she said 'Dear everyone' __________
  - 'How are you?' __________
  - 'I'm well' __________
  - 'from Simone' __________
- how Simone signed off her letter __________
- where she put the date __________

まんが に ついて

A Read the まんが in 第二課 of your textbook. Choose the correct answer from the box in each statement and highlight it.

1 Amandaさん は [Maikuくん / ゆうこさん / おばあさん] にでんわ を しました。

2 はなこさん は Chappii と [しゅくだい を して います。 / べんきょう して います。 / あそんで います。]

3 [Chappii / Maikuくん / Amandaさん] は せ が たかい です。

4 Amandaさん は すぐ [うみ / ゆうこさん の うち / Maikuくん の うち] に いきました。

5 Chappii は [あし が みじかい / みみ が ちいさい / め が おおきい] です。

6 Maikuくん は [きれい / hansamu / せ が ひくい] です。

7 Amandaさん は [Chappii / booru あそび / Maikuくん] が だいすき です。

第三課・へん じゃない ですよ。

ききましょう

A Can you identify who is speaking? Put a number in the box next to each character.

B Listen to the following people being interviewed about their nationality and what language they speak. In the table below, fill in where they are from and what language (or languages) they speak. They all speak日本語.

Name	*Country*	*Languages*
Paul		
Barbara		
Sri		
Mark		
Maria		

C Listen to these people talking and for each conversation highlight whether or not they are in agreement.

一	Agree	Disagree
二	Agree	Disagree
三	Agree	Disagree
四	Agree	Disagree
五	Agree	Disagree

D Listen to tomorrow's weather forecast for Japan. Draw a line between the name of the city and the appropriate weather symbol. Before starting, you may want to check the meaning of each symbol on 三十八ページ of the きもの 2 textbook.

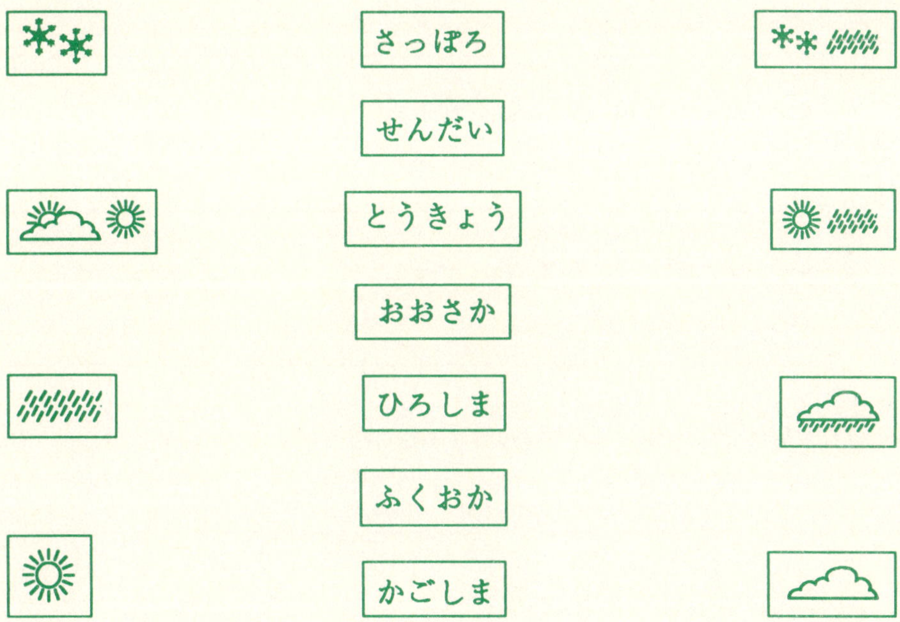

れんしゅう しましょう

A You have a friend who disagrees with you, no matter what you say. Write what she is likely to say when you make the following comments.

1 この ケーキ は おいしい ですね。

いいえ、おいしくない です。

2 この ハンバーガー は おおきい ですね。

3 この レストラン は しずか ですね。

4 この ビデオ は へん ですね。

5 カイリーさん は ゆうめい ですね。

6 その おんがく は うるさい です。

7 せいじくん は ハンサム ですね。

8 カタカナ は やさしい ですね。

9 いもうと の へや は きたない です。

B You really don't feel like doing anything much today. Choose an excuse from the list below that would be an appropriate response to the invitations that your energetic friends are giving.

みみ が いたいん です。
おもしろくない です。
め が いたいん です。
あし が いたいん です。
かぜ を ひいて います。
あぶない です。
うま は いや です。

1 テニス を しませんか。

You: テニス? ______________________________

2 ビデオ を みませんか。

You: ビデオ ですか。 ______________________________

3 じょうば スクール に いきませんか。

You: じょうば ですか。 ______________________________

4 ローラースケート を しませんか。

You: ローラースケート は あんまり... ______________________________

5 スクーバ ダイビング を しませんか。

You: スクーバ ダイビング? ______________________________

6 クラシック おんがく を ききませんか。

You: クラシック おんがく ですか。 ______________________________

C マークくん is staying with a Japanese family. He is having a bit of trouble getting some of his expressions right. Look at each incident below and, in the space provided, write what he should have said.

1 As he left to go to school this morning, he said 「いってらっしゃい」to his host mother. She looked surprised!

____

2 His school friend complimented him on his 日本語 and he replied 「ありがとう」

____

3 When he started his lunch, he said「ごちそうさま」.

____

4 マークくん went to his friend's place after school. He said 「おじゃましました」 as he went in.

____

5 マークくん was enjoying some cake with his friend and he said 「まずいですね」.

____

6 When he returned to his host family's home, he said「いってきます」.

____

7 On his way to bed, マークくん said「こんばん は」to everyone.

____

D When you find yourself sitting next to the Japanese exchange student on the school bus, you decide to try out your 日本語. What will you say in each situation below?

1 You comment on the great weather.

□□□□□○□□□。

2 You want to find out where she lives.

○□□□□□□□□□。

3 You want to find out what year level she is in.

○□□□□□□□□。

4 You want to invite her to watch a video at your house tomorrow.

□□□□□□□□□□○□□□□。

5 You compliment her on her English!

○□□□□□□□□□□。

Transfer the ひらがな in the circled boxes to the boxes below and you will discover the exchange student's name.

○○ ○○○

E The weather bureau has issued the following weather forecast (てんき よほう) for tomorrow. Your job is to prepare the weather report for the 七じのニュース. Use the same symbols as the ones on 三十八ページ of your textbook. Mark in the names of all the cities mentioned in the report.

てんき よほう
あしたの てんき です。

きゅうしゅう ちほう、かごしま は くもり のち はれ でしょう。かごしま の さいこうきおん は 13ど でしょう。ふくおか は あめ のち ゆき でしょう。さいこうきん は 7ど でしょう。
ほんしゅう の おてんき です。ひろしま はくもり でしょう。いちにちじゅう さむい でしょう。さいこうきおん は 6ど です。おおさか の あした の てんき は はれ でしょう。さいこうきおん は 11ど でしょう。とうきょう の あした の おてんき は はれ、さいこうきおん は 9ど でしょう。せんだい は はれ のち くもり でしょう。さいこうきおん は 4ど でしょう。
ほっかいどう ちほう、さっぽろ は ゆき、そして さいこうきおん は 2ど でしょう。

ちほう—area　さいこうきおん—maximum temperature　いちにちじゅう—all day

F Below is a transcript of an interview recorded with Natalie, an exchange student studying in Japan. Use the information gathered by the reporter to write an article about Natalie for the Japanese school newspaper.

REPORTER: おなまえは なんですか。
ナタリ: ナタリ です。
REPORTER: どこ から きましたか。
ナタリ: オーストラリア から きました。
REPORTER: いつ ここ に きましたか。
ナタリ: 一月 に きました。
REPORTER: なに語 を はなしますか。
ナタリ: オーストラリアで えい語 を はなします。
REPORTER: なんさい ですか。
ナタリ: 十五さい です。
REPORTER: なんねんせい ですか。
ナタリ: こうこう 一ねんせい です。
REPORTER: ひまなとき なに を しますか。
ナタリ: ともだちと あそびます。そして うちで レコード を ききます。
REPORTER: おんがく は すき ですか。
ナタリ: はい、だい すき です。ロック が すき です。
REPORTER: いつ オーストラリア に かえりますか。
ナタリ: 十二月 に かえります。

タスク

A group of Japanese students is coming to your school for a homestay (ホーム・ステー). In your notebook, draw up a schedule for them according to the program below.

They will arrive at your school by bus at about 3.00p.m. You could then have a welcome party or a meeting where each student is introduced to the homestay family with whom they will spend the evening.

The following day will be spent at your school. The students will have an English lesson and perhaps visit some other classes. In the afternoon they would like to play some sport or shop or have free time. In the evening you are planning a party.

The group will depart at 9.00a.m. the next day. They will meet at school where you will farewell them.

On 四十五 ページ of your textbook are schedules which you can refer to for ideas. You might also like to include symbols for some of the activities on the schedule.

日本 に ついて

On a visit to Japan, you won your choice of the holiday packages advertised on 四十五 ページ of your textbook.

Write to your friends at home telling them about your win and which holiday you chose. Also tell them about how you got there, where you stayed, what you did (they'll be really interested in a detailed breakdown) and how much you learnt.

漢字 と カタカナ

人	人 (stroke order 1, 2)
Meaning: *person*	
Readings ひと じん、にん (り)	
この人 (このひと) 日本人 (にほんじん) 三人 (さんにん)　二人 (ふたり)	

語	語 (stroke order 1–14)
Meaning: *language*	
Readings ご	
日本語 (にほんご) 単語 (たんご) フランス語 (フランスご)	

人 人 人
人 人
語 語 語 語 語 語
語 語 語 語 語 語
語 語 語
語 語

れんしゅう

A For the jamboree, each scout had to fill in a form giving their name, nationality and language. This information can be found on 三十五 ページ of your textbook. As the organizer of the jamboree, collate this information in かんじ, ひらがな and カタカナ on the chart below.

	Name	Nationality	Language
Hideo		日本人	日本語
Mei			
Mario			
Helga			
Mark			
Barbara			
Scott			
Sri			

B Complete the information about はなこさん and ゆうこさん in かんじ.

ゆうこさん は ＿＿＿＿＿ (Japanese) です。はなこさん も ＿＿＿＿＿ (Japan)

から きました。はなこさん も ゆうこさん も ＿＿＿＿＿ (Japanese)

を はなします。＿＿＿＿＿ (December) に かぞくと ＿＿＿＿＿ (Japan)

に かえりました。

いま ゆうこさん は えい＿＿＿＿＿ (English) の ＿＿＿＿＿ (book) を よんで

います。

C The designer of this tourist brochure quit suddenly, leaving the job incomplete. Write beside each symbol the correct word, choosing from the list of activities below. When you have done that, sketch symbols for the activities that remain and then add the word for the activity in order to complete the brochure.

サイクリング	ゴルフ
フィッシング	テニス
スキー	カヌー・ボート
ハイキング	ヘリコプター

This heading is also part of the tourist brochure. What is its purpose?

プランニングシート

まんが に ついて

A Read the まんが in 第三課 of your textbook. Choose the correct answer from the boxes in each statement and highlight it.

1 [ホセくん / はなこさん / チャッピー] は びょうき です。

2 みんな は [おみまい / がっこう / としょかん] に いきました。

3 はなこさん は [かぜ を ひいて います。 / ラジオ を きいて います。 / テニス を して います。]

4 イタリア で は [フランス語 / イタリア語 / えい語] を はなします。

5 [あたらしい / つまらない / むずかしい] ファミコンゲーム を しました。

6 [ホセくん / ジアングくん / はなこさん] は うち に かえりました。

7 [アマンダさん / せんせい / ゆうこさん] は ファミコン が すき です。

第四課・チャッピー！こら！

ききましょう

A はなこさん and ゆうこさん are talking about チャッピー. Write the かんじ number in the box next to the picture which best illustrates where he is.

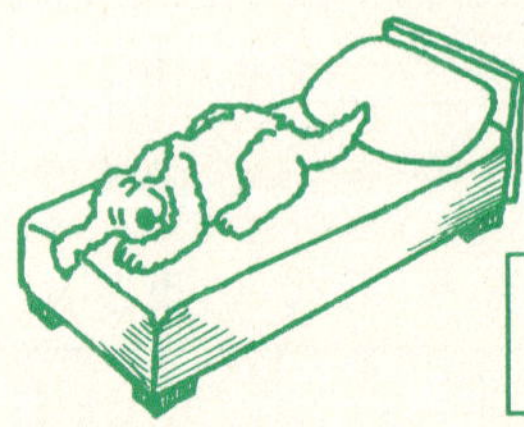

B Listen to part of a survey being carried out at a school to find out how many pets the students have. Assist in the collection of the information by writing in either the numbers of animals as you hear them, or by circling 'No pets', whichever is appropriate.

ペットのアンケート					

Jenny					No pets
Michael					No pets
Anne					No pets
Chris					No pets
Ben					No pets
Michelle					No pets
John					No pets

C Eliminator ゲーム

You will hear three statements for each set of pictures. As you listen to each statement, you will find that one picture does not fit — cross it out. When you have eliminated three pictures, you will be left with a picture that best illustrates the information given in the statements.

1    

2    

3    

4    

れんしゅう しましょう

A An important part of the job of the nurse who works for the vet in the cartoon story is to keep track of where all the animals are at the beginning of the day. She has to complete an animal inventory form. Because she is sick today, you are taking her place and completing the form.

	Animal Inventory	Day	
	Number	Location	Total number
いぬ	一ぴき	つくえ の したに います。	
ねこ			
へび			
かめ			
さる			

B What terrible luck! On the first morning of the Japanese language camp, you have fallen ill. You will have to have special excuse slips signed by the camp supervisor, which you present to the various activity leaders in order to exempt you from the activities. The supervisor will sign slips only if they are in good 日本語.

(Note: When you are writing about aches and pains, ん is not used. For example, おなか が いたいん です is used in speech but おなか が いたい です is the correct written form.)

1 I am not swimming today — I have a sore throat.

2 I am not horse-riding today — I have a headache.

3 I am not doing judo — I am sick.

4 I am not going cycling — I have a stomach-ache.

C Answer these questions about yourself (よく means *often*).

1 よく コーヒー を のみますか。

2 よく ハンバーガー を たべますか。

3 よく くるま を あらいますか。

4 ピアノ を ひきますか。

5 よく てがみ を かきますか。

6 よく しんぶん を よみますか。

7 よく としょかんに いきますか。

8 けんどう を しますか。

D Some of the Japanese students visiting your school on the homestay program will be visiting your class. To help you prepare for their visit, work out at least eight questions that you can ask the students. You could ask them about their family, pets, spare-time activities, sport...

1 ____________________

2 ____________________

3 ____________________

4 ____________________

5 ____________________

6 ____________________

7 ____________________

8 ____________________

E Your friend, Jamie, has finally made time to reply to his pen-friend, こうじ. He is sending the family photo below and wants you to write a short description of each family member and the dog in the photo. (Jamie is the person in the doorway going off to play soccer.)

F When you are giving a じこしょうかい, you can also include information about your family and pets. Using the family information on 五十五ページ of your textbook as a reference, write out information about your family.

タスク

The animal refuge centre in よこはま has too many pets. Choose one or two pets and design a newspaper advertisement to encourage people to adopt the featured pet(s).

Your advertisement could include a description of the animal, its name and a drawing of it.

日本 に ついて

A That instant expert family friend who visited 日本 recently is at it again! Now he is telling everyone all sorts of stories about the pop music industry in Japan. See if you can set him straight by writing a response to each of his statements below.

1 Young people in Japan mainly listen to music sung by overseas groups.

____

2 Japanese bands like to create a かわいい image and are generally pretty straight!

____

3 All pop music in Japan is sung by アイドル かしゅ.

____

B Below are the names, in カタカナ, of some overseas singers and groups who are popular in Japan. Try to work out their names.

1 マドンナ ______________________________

2 カイリー・ミノーグ ______________________________

3 デュランデュラン ______________________________

4 ザ・ビートルズ ______________________________

5 ボン ジョビ ______________________________

6 ニューキッズ (オンザブロック) ______________________________

7 ビリー・ジョエル ______________________________

8 マイケル・ジャクソン ______________________________

漢字 と カタカナ

父	母	何
Meaning: *father*	Meaning: *mother*	Meaning: *what?*
Readings ちち (お)とう(さん)	Readings はは (お)かあ(さん)	Readings なに、なん
父 (ちち) お父さん (おとうさん)	母 (はは) お母さん (おかあさん)	何語 (なにご) 何人 (なんにん)

父

母

何

父 父 父 父 父
父 父

母 母 母 母 母 母
母 母

何 何 何 何 何 何
何 何 何 何

れんしゅう

A Write these words in ひらがな. (There may be more boxes than you need.)

お母さん

父

何語

何人

お父さん

母

何月

B ティムくん is not very confident about writing in かんじ and カタカナ. He has written a letter to his pen-friend, えりこさん, and given you an English copy of what he wants to say. Fill in the missing parts for him with the correct かんじ and カタカナ.

There are three people in my family. My dad's name is Elio. My mum's name is Jan. My mum is an Australian and my dad is Italian. At home we speak English and Italian. And I'm studying Japanese at school! What languages do you speak, Eriko? How many people are there in your family?

かぞくは ________ です。________ のなまえは __________

です。__________ のなまえは ______________ です。

________ は ______________ で、________ は __________

です。うちで えい__________ も __________もはなします。

ぼくはがっこうで __________ をべんきょう

しています。

えりこさんは ____________ を はなしますか。ごかぞくは

____________ ですか。

C A cutting about Yoko Tanaka from a magazine is reproduced on 五十八ページ of your textbook. Below is a list of the promotional give-aways to celebrate 'Yoko day'. Write beside each one what it is.

B2 ポスター ____________________

ようこの T・シャツ ____________________

プロフィール ビデオ ____________________

オリジナルテレホンカード ____________________

コンサートの チケット ____________________

ようこ の バッジ ____________________

D A カタカナ character is 'concealed' in each of the illustrations below. Find each character, highlight it and then label each illustration using the highlighted character as the first letter of each word.

	ン	デ	ィ	ア	ン

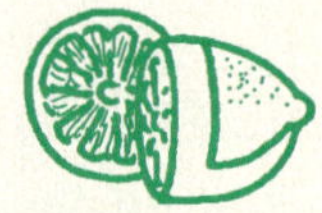

まんが に ついて

A Read the まんが in 第四課 of your textbook and then decide whether the following statements are true or false. Write まる(O) if the statement is true and ばつ(X) if it is false.

1 チャッピーとはなこさんは さんぽ に いきました。 _____

2 チャッピーは ヤミーを たべません。 _____

3 びょういんは とても こんでいます。 _____

4 はなこさん と ゆうこさん と チャッピーは 二じはん に びょういん に いきます。 _____

5 チャッピーは びょうき じゃないです。 _____

6 さる は きのうえ に います。 _____

7 ぶた は ベンチ の まえ に います。 _____

8 チャッピーは としちゃん の チョコレートを たべました。_____

B Look at the bottom cartoon frame on 四十七ページ and answer the following questions.

1 へび は 何びき いますか。 ________________

2 さる は この へや に いますか。 ________________

3 かめ は この へや に いますか。 ________________

4 いぬ は 何びき いますか。 ________________

5 ぶた は この へや に いますか。 ________________

6 ねこ は 何びき いますか。 ________________

7 ひつじ は 何びき いますか。 ________________

第五課・ドーナツ は ぜんぜん 食べません。

ききましょう

A Listen to what these people replied when asked the time. Write the number below the clock which shows the time.

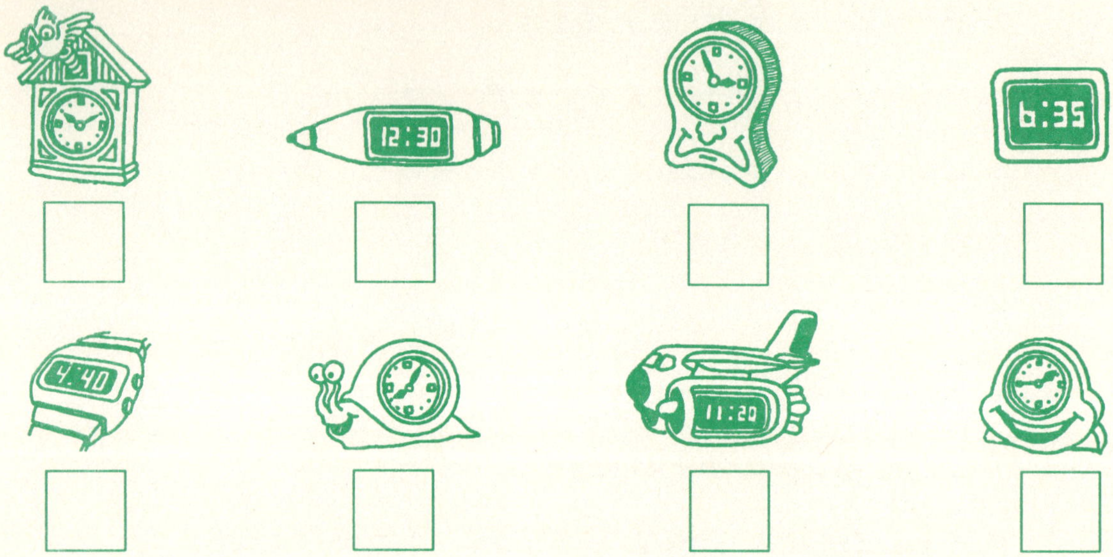

B Listen as your teacher reads out the program for the swimming sports. For each event, write in the distance to be swum.

freestyle	______________	メートル
relay	______________	メートル
back-stroke	______________	メートル
butterfly	______________	メートル
medley	______________	メートル
medley	______________	メートル

C Listen as these people are complimented on what they are wearing. Write the number next to the clothing which is commented on.

れんしゅう しましょう

A You are the compere of a fashion parade. Look at what the characters below are wearing and write down what you will say about each one. You can refer to 六十六ページ and 六十七ページ of your textbook for the names of clothing items.

1 一ばん は ホセくん です。
あたらしい スニーカー を はいています。そして すてきな
ポロシャツ を きています。

2 ______

3 ______

4 ______

5 ______

B You have decided to join Mike on his fitness program. Look at the schedule below and write down what your routine would be.

例:
まいあさ 六じ十ぷん に おきます。げつようびに 十キロ
はしって、七じ二十ぷんに うち に かえります。シャワーを
あびて、あさごはんを 食べます。それから 八じ五ふん まえ に
じてんしゃ で がっこう に 行きます。

C Your friend has asked you to be his coach for an athletics competition. You have written Week 1 of his program and now you want to step up his training. Write out his program for Week 2 and Week 3, making sure that it becomes progressively more challenging!

Week 1	Week 2	Week 3
七じ に おきます		
一キロ はしります		
げつようび に 50 メートル およぎます		
ときどき エアロビクス を します		
十五キロ サイクリング を します		

D Answer the following questions for each of the illustrations below.

a いま 何じ ですか。
b 何 を して いますか。

E You have a wardrobe full of clothes and shoes. Write what you plan to wear at the places or events illustrated.

1 やまで パーカ を きます。ジーンズを はきます。

2 ______________________________

3 ______________________________

4 ______________________________

5 ______________________________

6 ______________________________

F Some people say things like, 'I never watch TV', or 'I never study'. However, when you see them doing just that, they modify their statement and say, 'I occasionally do...', or 'I sometimes do...'
Anticipate what these people may say after being caught doing the activities illustrated.

1 わたし は ぜんぜん テレビ を みません。

____

2 ぼく は ぜんぜん コーヒー を のみません。

____

3 ぼく は ぜんぜん しゅくだい を しません。

____

4 わたし は ぜんぜん マクドナルド で 食べません。

____

5 わたし は ぜんぜんワンピース を きません。

____

G This is a magazine article about Florence Joiner. Read the article and see if you can answer the questions that follow.

1988 ねん のソウルオリンピック、ながい かみ と きれいな メークアップ、28 さい の アメリカ人、 フロレンス・ジョイナーは 100メートル と 200メートル の ゴールド・メダリスト です。 ジョイナー は せが たかくて、ながい ゆび に マニキュア を していました。

ジョイナーの ハード な トレーニング は ゆうめい です。まいにち エアロビクス を して、50キロ の バーベル で ウェート リフティング を れんしゅう しました。プール で 1000メートル およいで、20キロ サイクリング を しました。

アイスクリームと ケーキ は ぜんぜん 食べませんでした。ピザ と ハンバーガー も あまり 食べませんでした。ジョイナー の あさごはん は オレンジ・ジュース、ハイ ファイバー・シリアル と ミルク でした。

つらい トレーニング に たえて、ジョイナー は オリンピック の ヒロイン に なりました。

せがたかくて・tall and... つらい・hard
たえて・endure なりました・became

1 In which Olympic Games did Florence Joiner participate?

2 Describe Florence Joiner (e.g. age, nationality, appearance).

3 In what events did she participate?

4 Describe her training program.

5 What was her diet while she was training?

タスク

You will be the host to one of the students coming to your school on the homestay program. As your guest will be arriving soon, you have agreed to send off a letter to help prepare him or her. You will need to include the following information:

- where you live;
- details about each member of the family, including their names, ages, something about their appearances, what they like to do;
- what pets, if any, you have;
- what season it is during the time of their visit and what the weather will be like;
- what you usually do or like to do in that season.

If there is anything else you would like to tell your guest, include that also.

日本 に ついて

A After reading in your きもの 2 textbook about the school year in Japan (七十 ページ and 七十一 ページ) and about the seasons (六十八 ページ), decide when you would choose to do a one-month school visit to Japan. (Consider such things as the weather, activities related to the season and school events.)

After you have decided what time of the year would be best, write out all the reasons for your choice in your notebook.

B You have a new job in a travel agency giving advice to people who want to travel to Japan. In which month would you advise the people below to go?

1 Mr and Mrs Rose want to see the cherry blossoms. ______________

2 John Walker wants to hike to the top of Mt Fuji. ______________

3 Melissa White is a keen skier. ______________

4 Mike Frame is a physical education teacher who wants to watch school sporting activities. ______________

5 Mrs Wright doesn't like weather which is either very hot or very cold and she is interested in gardening. ______________

漢字 と カタカナ

行	
Meaning: *go*	
Readings い (きます)	
行きます(いきます) 行って (いって)	

食	
Meaning: *eat*	
Readings た(べます)	
食べます (たべます) 食べて (たべて)	

れんしゅう

A Give ひらがな readings for these かんじ.

食べます		四人	
行きます		四月	
お父さん		日本語	
お母さん		三百	
何人		七百	
二人		日本人	

B Rewrite the short conversations below, changing the underlined words to かんじ.

「まいにち なんじ に あさごはん を たべますか。」
「しちじ じゅうごふん に たべます。」
「なに を たべますか。」
「トースト を たべます。」

「なんがつ に にほん に いきましたか。」
「しがつ に いきました。」

「ごかぞく は なんにん ですか。」
「ろくにん です。あね が ふたり、いもうと が ひとり います。そして いぬ を さんびき かって います。ちち と はは は いま にほん に います。」
「ああ、そう ですか。」

C In the list below, highlight the items of clothing you have in your wardrobe.

ジージャン	パジャマ	ジーンズ
T・シャツ	セーター	ワンピース
ハイソックス	トレーニングシューズ	シャツ
ベルト	ショートパンツ	ブラウス
スカーフ	トレーナー	カーディガン
スカート	パーカ	スリッパ

まんが に ついて

A Read the まんが in 第語課 of your textbook and then highlight or circle the correct answer from the choices offered below each question.

1 アマンダさんは 何 を 食べて いますか。

2 マイクくんは まいあさ 何じ に おきますか。

3 マイクくんは プールで 何メートルおよぎますか。

 25メートル  300メートル

 100メートル  200メートル

4 マイクくんは あさごはんに 何 を 食べますか。

5 日よう日に みんなはどこに 行きましたか。

第六課・ベビーシッター は らくだなあ!

ききましょう

A えりさん has drawn the symbols below as an assignment for her graphics class and is explaining what they represent. Write the number of the sentence next to the symbol.

B Listen to these conversations as students ask permission to do various things. For each conversation, highlight with your マジック whether permission was given or refused.

1	Allowed	Not allowed
2	Allowed	Not allowed
3	Allowed	Not allowed
4	Allowed	Not allowed
5	Allowed	Not allowed
6	Allowed	Not allowed

C ひろしくん's parents are going out tonight and he and his friend, いちろうくん, are staying home by themselves. His father tells him what he is permitted (or not permitted) to do. Mark ✓ beside each picture if he has been given permission and X if he is not allowed to do what is shown in the illustration.

れんしゅう しましょう

A Lee and Emmy's parents have asked you to baby-sit for them. You know what happened to Terry when he looked after Lee and Emmy, so you have decided to set down the house rules clearly. Under each illustration, write an appropriate rule.

B Give an honest opinion of how much you like (or dislike) the following things.

1 くろい ジーンズ は すき ですか。

____

2 スモーキーカラーの T・シャツ は すき ですか。

____

3 ホットドッグ は すき ですか。

____

4 がっこう の せいふく は すき ですか。

____

5 ザ・ビートルズ(The Beatles)の うた は すき ですか。

____

6 ねこ は すき ですか。

____

C Your friend ひろし is looking for two other people to share his house. He has written out most of the advertisement but has asked you to help him with the 'conditions' section. Write the conditions in the spaces left in the advertisement.

To Let

2 rooms in a large house near the university.

Conditions:

______________________ でんわ を つかって も いい です。

______________________ テレビ を 見て も いい です。

______________________ ペット を かって は だめ です。

______________________ ビール を のんで は だめ です。

______________________ ピアノ を ひいて も いい です。

______________________ プール で およいで も いい です。

Rent $100/week. Call Hiroshi after 6.00p.m. on 777 0070

D It is time to practise making the て form of verbs again. Complete the table below.

Weak	て form	Strong	て form
食べます		かえります	
あけます		はしります	
でかけます		つくります	
ねます		はいります	
おきます		あいます	
見ます		買います	
あびます		つかいます	
きます(wear)		かきます	
		はきます	
		およぎます	

E You have a job assisting the きもの illustrator. Your assignment is to colour the まんが according to the instructions below.

1 ホセくん は あかい ポロシャツ を きて います。
2 ゆうこさん は あおい カーディガン を きて います。
3 せんせい の ワンピース は ブルー です。 くつ も ブルー です。
4 アマンダさん の ブラウス は ピンク です。
5 はなこさん の T・シャツ は オレンジ です。
6 マイクくん の ジャケット は みどり です。きいろい スニーカー を はいて います。ジーンズ は ブラック です。

F Choose an appropriate expression from the box below to complete each speech bubble.

だめ!	そう ですか。	そう でも ない です。
どうぞ	ひどい!	へえ?

タスク

You were one of the students surveyed at 東京 ディズニーランド. The survey results are on 八十四 ページ of your textbook. Write a letter to your friends back home telling them about your visit to Disneyland. Tell them who went with you, what you did, how much you spent and what you bought.

日本 に ついて

Simone, in her letter on 八十七 ページ, makes the following comment about all the new high-tech products: 'Sometimes I wonder about it all, but I suppose it all helps to make life better. What do you think?'

What *do* you think? Organise a debate (とうろんかい) to discuss whether the products that Simone has shown you would make life better. Below is a product list to assist you in your assessment.

パーティカラオケ
ビデオウォークマン
ラップトップワープロ
コピーペン
カラービデオプリンター
パームトップコンピューター

漢字 と カタカナ

見	見 (stroke order 1–7)

Meaning: *look, watch, see*

Readings
み (ます)

見ます (みます)
見て (みて)

見

買	買 (stroke order 1–12)

Meaning: *buy*

Readings
か (います)

買います (かいます)
買って (かって)

買

見 見 見 見 見 見
見 見
見 見

買 買 買 買 買 買
買 買 買 買 買 買
買 買 買

れんしゅう

A Using かんじ, complete the sentences below each picture.

まちに ___ きました。

えいがを ___ ました。

おかしを ___ いました。

おかしを ___ べました。

レストランに ___ きました。

ピザを ___ べました。

ファミコンゲームを ___ ました。

ファミコンゲームを ___ いました。

B Draw a line matching the かんじ word to its ひらがな reading.

日本人	みます
お母さん	いきます
六月	なんがつ
食べます	かいます
見ます	なにご
買います	にほんじん
行きます	おかあさん
何語	おとうさん
お父さん	ろくがつ
何月	たべます

C Many Japanese magazines feature clothing that is in the latest エコロジーカラー. Fill in the colour guide below according to the colour given.

☐	カーキ	☐	サンド ベージュ
☐	オリーブ グリーン	☐	レイク ブルー
☐	ロック ブラウン	☐	ミルク ホワイト
☐	アフリカン オレンジ	☐	マイルド レッド
☐	レモン イエロー	☐	スモーキー ピンク

まんが に ついて

A The following statements refer to the まんが in 第六課 of your textbook. Decide which of the alternatives — a, b or c — best tells what is happening. Circle the letter of the sentence you choose.

1 a テリーくんは トレーニングをします。
b テリーくんは ベビーシッター を します。
c こどもたち は ベビーシッター を します。

2 a こどもたち は いつも 七じはん に ごはん を 食べます。
b こどもたち は いつも 七じはん に シャワー を あびます。
c こどもたち は いつも 七じはん におふろ に はいります。

3 リーちゃんと エミちゃんのルール (rule):
a テレビ の へや で 食べても いい です。
b ボール あそび を して は だめ です。
c おふろ に はいって は だめ です。

4 a リーちゃん と エミちゃん は おふろ で シャンプー を つかって います。
b リーちゃん と エミちゃん は おふろ で ファミコン を して います。
c リーちゃん と テリーくん は おふろ で シャンプー を つかって います。

5 a リーちゃん は あおい パジャマ が すき です。
b エミちゃん は きいろい パジャマ が すき です。
c リーちゃん は あかい パジャマ が きらい です。

6 a テリーくん は ボール あそび を して います。
b テリーくん は ホットケーキ を 食べて います。
c テリーくん は ばん ごはん を 食べて います。

7 a リーちゃん と エミちゃん は 十一じ 二十五ふん に ねました。
b リーちゃん と エミちゃん は 十二じ 二十五ふん に ねました。
c テリーくん と リーちゃん は 十一じ 二十五ふん に ねました。

第七課・このいすのあしはありますか。

ききましょう

A Listen to these people talking and decide in which shop the conversation is taking place. Write the number of the sentence in the circle above the shop.

B The owner of the クール・コーヒーショップ is impressed with your 日本語 and has employed you as a waiter/waitress. As the customers give you their orders, keep a tally of the number of items ordered and then write the total next to each item.

たべもの		Total	のみもの		Total
ハム サンドイッチ			コーヒー 		
チーズ サンドイッチ			アイス コーヒー		
サラダ			レモン ティー		
ピザ トースト 			ココア		
			ミルク		
チーズ ケーキ			コーラ		
クレープ			ジュース 		
アイスクリーム 			オレンジ		
			トマト		

C Listen to these people asking where various things are and put a ✓ in the box next to the picture which best illustrates where the item is.

D You have a holiday job working at the fruit shop. As the manager calls out the prices of the items, write them on the labels.

れんしゅう しましょう

A Read the statements below and decide which shopトムくん has been to.

1 パパイヤ を買いました。 ________ に 行きました。

2 チューリップを 買いました。 ________ に 行きました。

3 ふでばこ を 買いました。 ________ に 行きました。

4 サンドイッチを 買いました。 ________ に 行きました。

5 さしみ を 買いました。 ________ に 行きました。

6 じしょ を 買いました。 ________ に 行きました。

7 アスパラガスを 買いました。 ________ に 行きました。

8 ソーセージを 買いました。 ________ に 行きました。

B The lost property office is overflowing with unnamed items. You have been asked to write up the list to put on the notice-board.

	Item	Number		Item	Number
5 dictionaries	じしょ	五さつ	7 rulers		
6 cassettes			9 notebooks		
9 erasers			2 maths books		
3 highlighter pens			15 pencils		
8 tennis balls			4 pencil cases		

C Your father couldn't stand your brother Mark's untidy room any longer so he tidied it up.

He thought that perhaps Mark would respond better to Japanese instructions than to English ones ー he has asked you to write where things are in 日本語 so that he can put the notice below on Mark's bedroom wall.

マーク の きれいな へや
ようふく は たんす のなか に あります。
バスケット ボール は ______________________ 。
テニス ラケット は ______________________ 。
スニーカー は ______________________ 。
えんぴつ は ______________________ 。
パジャマ は ______________________ 。
スケート ボード は ______________________ 。
スキー は ______________________ 。
本 は ______________________ 。
お父さん　より

D Your latest part-time job is writing labels at the fruit shop. The owner has given you the information and a sample of what he wants the labels to look like. Complete the remaining labels.

キーウィ フルーツ
10 コ
せんろっぴゃく えん

キーウィ
フルーツ
10 コ
1600 円

メロン
2 コ
きゅうせん はっぴゃく
えん

オレンジ
20 コ
さんぜんごひゃく えん

パパイヤ
5 コ
よんせんにひゃく えん

さくらんぼ
1kg
ななせんさんびゃく
えん

グレープ フルーツ
10 コ
にせん
ひゃくごじゅう えん

みかん
3kg
ごせんろっぴゃく
ごじゅう えん

E You are an *Ultraman* (ウルトラマン) comic fan. When you hear that your friend is going to Japan, you write down some Japanese expressions to enable him to buy comics for you.

1 Excuse me, where is the bookshop?

____

2 Do you have any *Ultraman* comics?

____

3 How much are they?

____

4 That's cheap.

____

5 I'll have six, please.

____

6 Thank you.

____

タスク

You'd really like to have breakfast at マクドナルド but you have to convince the others that there is something there they'd enjoy. Look at the メニュー on 九十九ページ of your textbook and write down what each person can look forward to eating and drinking.

1 Mum is a vegetarian.

____

2 Dad doesn't like eggs.

____

3 Big brother likes a full breakfast.

____

4 Big sister has a sweet tooth.

____

5 Little sister hates sweet things.

____

日本 に ついて・日本料理(りょうり)

すきやき を つくりましょう

1 electric frypan
1 large serving dish
6 small bowls
6 sets of chopsticks

ざいりょう for 六人
750g topside or sirloin beef, sliced very thinly
4 leeks, washed and sliced diagonally
8 mushrooms, criss-crossed on top with a knife
1 packet of はるさめ or しらたき noodles, parboiled
(vermicelli noodles may be substituted)
300g Chinese cabbage, sliced into 4cm lengths
300g tofu, cut into 4cm cubes
2 medium carrots, sliced thinly

すきやき たれ (sauce)
1/2 cup light soy sauce
1/2 cup みりん
1/2 cup だし
1 tablespoon sugar

つくりかた

1 Combine the sauce ingredients, bring to the boil and simmer for one minute. Place in a heat-resistant jug.
2 Arrange the other ingredients attractively on the large serving dish.
3 Brush the electric frypan with oil and heat to medium heat. Add half the beef, saute quickly and push to one side.
4 Add half the vegetables and other ingredients, keeping the different kinds of vegetables separate from each other.
5 Pour in half the sauce mixture and continue to cook over medium heat.
6 Each guest now breaks an egg into his or her bowl and beats it with chopsticks.
7 Each guest then helps him- or herself to meat and vegetables, dipping these into the egg to cool the hot meat and vegetables before eating.
8 Replenish the pan with meat, vegetables and sauce, as required.

おいしい ですね!

円 円

1 2 3 4

Meaning: *yen*

Readings

えん

百円 (ひゃく えん)
五円 (ごえん)

円 円 円 円 円

円 円

れんしゅう

A Complete the sentences below using かんじ and カタカナ.

__________ は __________ です。
banana　　ななひゃくえん

__________ は __________ _____ いました。
おかあさん　　ろっぽん　　か

__________ は __________ で
おかあさん　　resutoran

__________ を _____ べました。
sandoitchi　　た

__________ は __________ です。
sandoitchi　　さんびゃくろくじゅうえん

B Complete the tables of 'counters' below.

	なんにん
一人	
	ふたり
	さんにん
四人	
	ごにん
	ろくにん

何本	なんぼん
	いっぽん
	にほん
三本	
	よんほん
五本	
六本	

C The following extract is from the メニュー of a popular ice-cream shop. Arrange the flavours from 一 to 十, beginning with what you'd like to order first. Write both the カタカナ and English in your top ten.

フレーバー

チョコレート ミント
フレンチ バニラ
ブルーベリー チーズケーキ
ピスタチオ
グリーン ティー
ベリーベリー ストロベリー
ネオポリタン スワール
ラム レーズン
キャラメル リボン
ジャングル バナナ

一 ______________________ ______________________

二 ______________________ ______________________

三 ______________________ ______________________

四 ______________________ ______________________

五 ______________________ ______________________

六 ______________________ ______________________

七 ______________________ ______________________

八 ______________________ ______________________

九 ______________________ ______________________

十 ______________________ ______________________

まんが に ついて

A Read the まんが in 第七課 of your textbook and then decide whether the following statements are true or false. Write まる(O) if the statement is true and ばつ(X) if it is false.

1 ゆうこさん と はなこさん は ガレージ セール で ゴルフ ボール を うります。 ____

2 ランプシェード は アマンダさん の つくえ の うえ に あります。 ____

3 ホセくん は ベッド を うりました。 ____

4 くま の て は ありません。 ____

5 ふるい たんす は アンチック です。 ____

6 ふるい たんす は テリーくん の お母さん の たんす です。 ____

B Which character is being referred to in the following statements? Write his or her name in the space provided.

1 ゴルフクラブ を うりました。 ____________

2 でんき スタンド を うりました。 ____________

3 うえき を うりました。 ____________

4 ふるい たんす を うりました。 ____________

5 いす を うりました。 ____________

6 くま を うりました。 ____________

第八課・はし が つかえますか。

ききましょう

A はなこさん and ゆうこさん are answering questions about what implements are commonly used in Japan to eat certain foods. As you hear their explanations, put a ✓ in the space under the implement mentioned.

さしみ				
カレーライス				
アイスクリーム				
やきそば				
ピザ				
ステーキ				

B The committee elected to organize the end-of-the-year party are holding a meeting. Listen as they work out who is going to do what and draw a line from the member's name to the illustration representing their task.

パーティーコミッティー

れんしゅう しましょう

A Your bragging friend is at it again. Whatever you say you can do, he claims that he can do better. Anticipate his responses to the statements below.

1 ローマじ で てがみ が かけます。

RESPONSE: ひらがな と カタカナ で てがみ が かけますよ。

2 かんじ が 20 よめます。

RESPONSE: ________________________________

3 日本語 が すこし できます。

RESPONSE: ________________________________

4 ファミコン が つかえます。

RESPONSE: ________________________________

5 はし で スパゲッティー が 食べられます。

RESPONSE: ________________________________

6 ビール が のめます。

RESPONSE: ________________________________

7 スキー が できます。

RESPONSE: ________________________________

8 エレクトーン が ひけます。

RESPONSE: ________________________________

9 あさ の 五じ に おきられます。

RESPONSE: ________________________________

B Complete the table below.

Weak	
食べます	食べられます
あけます	
でかけます	
きます	
Strong	
はしります	
つくります	
つかいます	
買います	
うたいます	

かきます	
ひきます	
およぎます	
あそびます	
よみます	
のみます	
はなします	
Irregular	
きます	
行きます	
します	

C Your friend Jamie and his parents are going to 日本 for a holiday. Jamie is going to stay with his pen-friend こうじくん for two nights. Jamie has been trying to teach himself some 日本語. He knows the expressions below but is unsure when to use them. Write down for him when he would use these expressions.

1 おじゃまします。____________________

2 いただきます。____________________

3 おいしい です。____________________

4 おかえりなさい。____________________

5 いいえ、そうでも ないです。____________________

6 あんまりすき じゃないです。____________________

7 いいえ、むずかしくない です。____________________

D Jamie's parents would like your help too. They ask you to write out some useful phrases for them.

1 Excuse me, where is a bakery?

____

2 Do you speak English?

____

3 I can't speak Japanese.

____

4 I'm sorry, I don't understand.

____

5 I can't use chopsticks.

____

6 It's very hot today, isn't it?

____

7 Your English is very good.

____

8 May I have two iced coffees, please.

____

9 How much is this?

____

10 We're from Australia.

____

11 Excuse me, what time is it?

____

12 Thank you very much.

____

E Sometimes when you are listening in on someone's phone call, you can guess what is being said on the other end of the line. Below you will find カイリー's conversation. In the spaces, fill in what you think 本田くん might be saying.

カイリー・ホーガン

本田けんじ

カイリー: もしもし。

けんじ: ______________________________

カイリー: はい、そうです。あ、けんじくんですね。

けんじ: ______________________________

カイリー: おすし ですか。はい、食べられます。だいすきです。

けんじ: ______________________________

カイリー: こんばん は ちょっと...

けんじ: ______________________________

カイリー: あした ですか。いい ですよ。

けんじ: ______________________________

カイリー: レストランの まえ で あいましょう。

けんじ: ______________________________

カイリー: 七じはんに あいましょう。

けんじ: ______________________________

カイリー: ええ、もちろん おはし が つかえますよ。

けんじ: ______________________________

カイリー: はい、あした あいましょう。

けんじ: ______________________________

カイリー: じゃあ ね。

F Answer the questions about yourself below.

1 はし が つかえますか。

____

2 カタカナ が かけますか。

____

3 フランス語 が すこし できますか。

____

4 日本語 の うた が うたえますか。

____

5 ローラースケート が できますか。

____

6 ケーキ が つくれますか。

____

7 ドイツ語の しんぶん が よめますか。

____

8 どんな スポーツ が できますか。

____

タスク

ホーム・ステー

You are to host a Japanese student for two weeks. Write to the student and tell him or her all about what to expect when he/she stays at your home. Include as much information as possible.

You will be able to introduce yourself and your family and to give some details about them. You should write about what you do on the weekend and in your spare time (sport, music etc.).

The student will probably be interested to know about what year level you are in, what subjects you are studying and what you are good at.

You should probably mention one or two of the family's favourite foods that the student will be able to try.

If you have any specific questions, now is a good time to find out — before the student arrives!

日本 に ついて

A postcard from Hokkaidoo
(ほっかいどう から の えはかぎ)

Make your friends feel envious by sending them a postcard from ほっかいどう. Below are some suggestions about what you might like to mention (you're sure to think of other things to add):

・where you went and what it is like there
・what you saw and did
・what you ate
・what souvenirs you bought
・how impressed they should be because you've been able to write this card in Japanese!

漢字 と カタカナ

川	田	山
Meaning: *river*	Meaning: *rice field*	Meaning: *mountain*
Readings かわ (がわ)	Readings た (だ)	Readings やま
ながい 川 (ながい かわ) 山川さん (やまかわさん)	山田 さん (やまださん) 本田さん (ほんださん)	たかい 山 (たかい やま)
 川	 田	 山

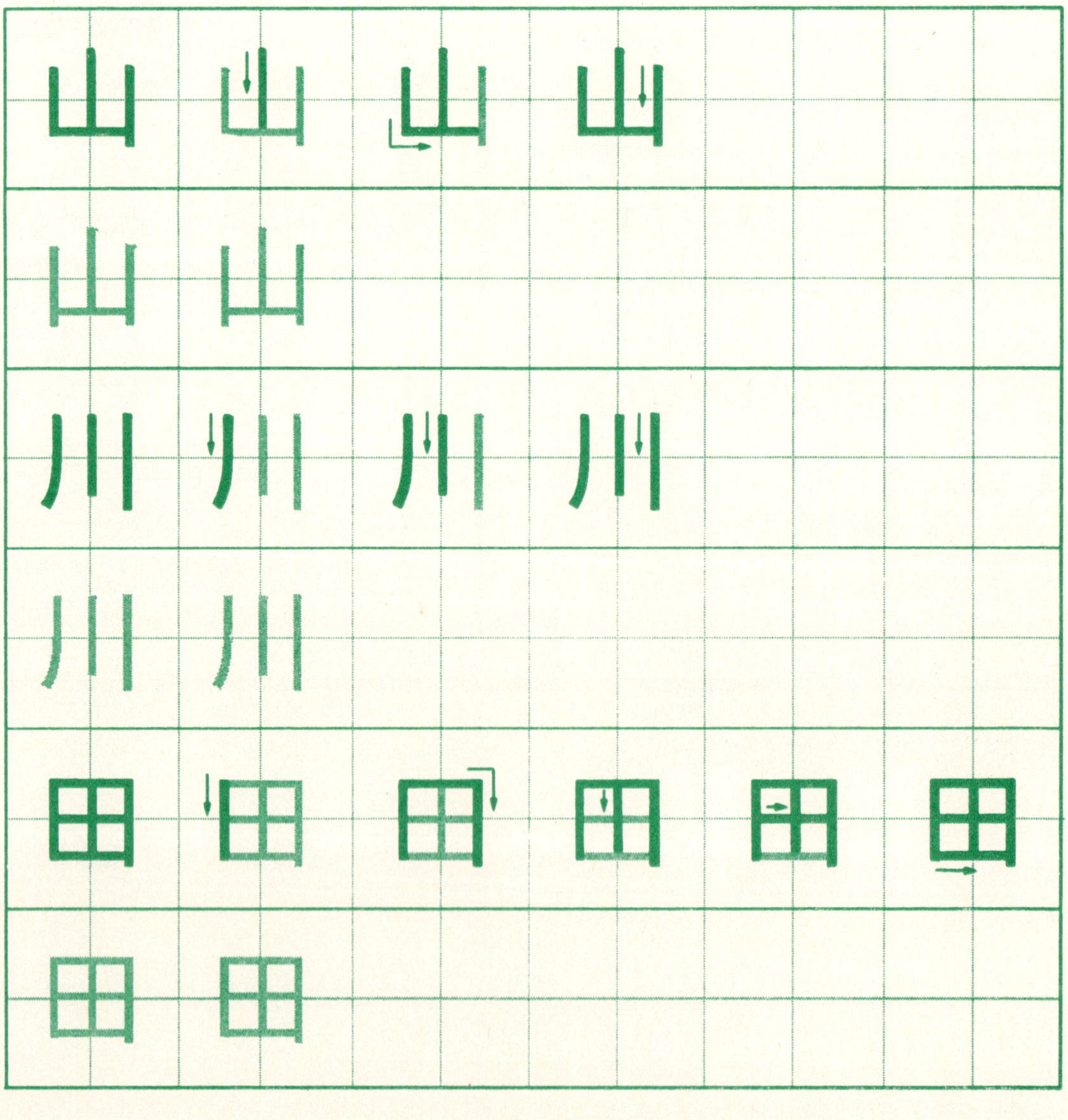

れんしゅう

A Complete the name-cards of the people below.
(Note: When 田 (た) is not the first character in a name, it is read as だ .)

B Draw a sketch to represent the meaning of the かんじ given below.

本

山

川

田

人

父と母

C Try to match each カタカナ ベビー word below to its English equivalent.

ベビーカー	a tiny camera
ベビーカメラ	baby-boom
ベビーゴルフ	a pram
ベビーベッド	mini-golf
ベビーブーム	a play-pen
ベビーサークル	a cot

D Try to guess the meanings of the ノー words below.

ノーアイロン ______________________________

ノーネクタイ ______________________________

ノースリーブ ______________________________

ノーコメント ______________________________

ノー・モア・ヒロツマ ______________________________

まんが に ついて

A Answer the questions below about the まんが in 第八課 of your textbook in complete Japanese sentences.

1 さくぶんを えんぴつで かいてもいい ですか。

____

2 さくぶん を ローマじ で かいてもいいですか。

____

3 さくぶん の だい は 何 ですか。

____

4 マイクくんは はし が つかえますか。

____

5 ホセくん は おりがみ が できますか。

____

6 ホセくん は おすし が 食べられますか。

____

7 ことし の がいじん 日本一 は だれ ですか。

____

8 ホセくん は さくぶん が ぜんぶ かけましたか。

____

きれいに かきましょう

日	日														
本	本														
月	月														
人	人														
語	語														
父	父														
母	母														
何	何														
行	行														
食	食														
見	見														
買	買														
円	円														
川	川														
田	田														
山	山														

You are able to make these sentences look more 'sophisticated' by rewriting each sentence and changing the underlined words into かんじ「漢字」。 You may have to add ひらがな to complete some words.

1 きのうまちにいって、ピザをたべました。

2 やまでへびをみましたよ。

3 じてんしゃでかわにいきましょう。

4 ごかぞくはなんにんですか。ごにんです。
ペットをかって　いますか。はい、いぬをにひきかっています。

5 ちちとははthan

6 きのうやおやでバナナをさんぼん　かいました。

7 やまださんはしがつにここにきました。しちがつににほんにかえります。

8 このほんはいくらですか。さんびゃくえんです。

パズル

This Wonderword contains only the names of countries. Fill in the ヒント section in English.

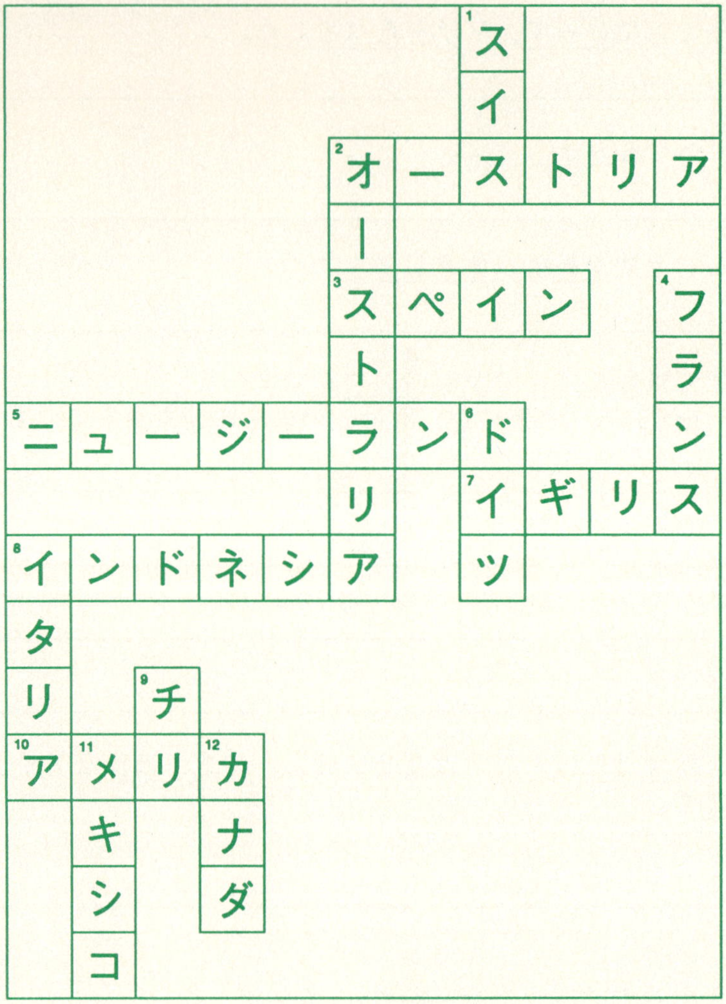

よこ (Across)

2 ______________________________

3 ______________________________

5 ______________________________

7 ______________________________

8 ______________________________

10 ______________________________

たて (Down)

1 ______________________________

2 ______________________________

4 ______________________________

6 ______________________________

8 ______________________________

9 ______________________________

11 ______________________________

12 ______________________________

The section that follows is 32 pages in length. You will need to turn to the last page of this workbbook and turn the book upside down in order to use this 32-page section.

F This is the breakfast menu on a flight to 東京 (とうきょう).
Useit as a reference to answer the questions below.

シンガポール・東京

朝食

ジュース

フレッシュフルーツ

A サーモンステーキ
トマトのグリル
マッシュルーム
ハッシュブラウンポテト

or

B スプリングオニオンとチキンオムレツ
トマトのグリル
マッシュルーム
ポテトのソテー

フルーツマフィン、ロールパン
バター、マーマレード

コーヒー 又は紅茶

1 Where did this flight begin? ________________

2 What will you begin your breakfast with? ________________

3 Which cooked course will you choose? ________________

What will be served to you? ________________

____

4 What is also served with this breakfast? ________________

5 You can have コーヒー or 紅茶 to drink. What do you think 紅茶 is?

________________ What will you have? ________________

D What is this leisure brochure advertising?

E What is being advertised here? What is its name?

れんしゅう しましょう

A What has the reopening of this store been called?

B What can you buy here?

スポーツコーナー

C What kind of resorts are being advertised? Where are they?

マウンテン　リゾート

カナダ・スイス

ニュージーランド

P カタカナ is used for the sounds of animals. Draw a line to match each sound to its appropriate animal. Sometimes they sound a little different to what you may think!

ヒヒーン	モーモー	コケコッコー	ニャーニャー	ワンワン	ブーブー

Q What would you do if you saw a パトカー through your バック ミラー?

ピーポーピーポー

____

____

R After you have found all the food items in the puzzle (horizontally and vertically) and crossed them out, two カタカナ will remain. They will spell out the Japanese word for 'bread'.

ト	ー	ス	ト	ア
チ	サ	ラ	ダ	イ
キ	チ	ピ	ザ	ス
ン	｜	ド	デ	ク
パ	ズ	｜	ザ	リ
ケ	ガ	ナ	｜	｜
｜	ム	ツ	ト	ム
キ	ン	ス	ー	プ

ヒント	
aisukuriimu	keeki
chiizu	piza
chikin	sarada
dezaato	suupu
doonatsu	toosuto
gamu	

'Bread' in 日本語 is ______________________________

M On page 二十九 of your textbook is a chart of created sounds. The words below use these sounds. Try to work out their meanings.

パーティー ____________ フォーク ____________

サーフィン ____________ ファミコン ____________

フェリーボート ____________ シェフ ____________

チェリー ____________ ジェットき ____________

ディズニーランド ____________ アイスティー ____________

N Your names are also written using many created sounds. From the class list given below, highlight either the names of the boys or the names of the girls.

ソフィー	クリストファー
ディーン	ミシェル
ウェイン	マーティン
シェーン	アンジェラ
ジェニファー	フィオナ
クリスティン	ジェームズ

O Each カタカナ word here is one of a pair, e.g. coffee - juice. Draw a line to connect each pair.

ジーンズ　ジュース　ピアノ　ニュージーランド

ビデオ　エアロビクス　ギター

テレビ　ペン　T. シャツ　スニーカー　ナイフ

シャワー　マジック　フォーク　ジョギング

シャンプー　オーストラリア　コーヒー　スリッパ

K　マクドナルド are promoting their products.

What is the promotion called? ______________________________

What are the presents? ______________________________

L　As you know, カタカナ, like ひらがな, uses little ヤ, ユ, and ヨ to create new sounds. Complete these words which use little ヤ, ユ or ヨ.

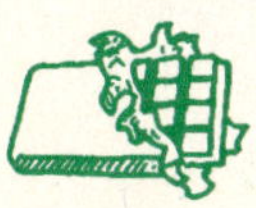

チ				ー	

ジ		

シ		

キ			

チ		ー	

ニ		ー		ー	

ジ		ー	

シ			ー

I See if you can you work out what the following words mean.

ウエートレス ______

ウインドー ______

ウインク ______

ウイスキー ______

Try writing these words.

ueetaa								
uiikuendo								
uootaa.poro						·		
uonbatto								

J Many famous Japanese brand names are often written in カタカナ.
Complete the list below.

YAMAHA				
TOYOTA				
KAWASAKI				
NIKON				

Now write the English for the カタカナ names below.

ナショナル ______

ソニー ______

セイコー ______

カシオ ______

G Label the stationery items using the words given in the box.

ノート　けしゴム　ペン　クレヨン　セロテープ　マジック

H Using the map on page 二十三 as a reference, fill in the boxes below with the names of the countries given.

アフリカ・AFRICA

Egypt

Kenya

アジア・ASIA

Indonesia

Saudi Arabia

U.S.S.R.

ヨーロッパ・EUROPE

Norway

Sweden

Yugoslavia

オセアニア・OCEANIA

Guam

Hawaii

Vanuatu

北［きた］アメリカ・NORTH AMERCIA

Mexico

You may have been puzzled when writing the カタカナ for 'Norway' and 'Sweden'. Both these countries' names have the sound *we* in their pronunciation. The sound *we* and also the sounds *wi* and *wo* have these variations:

ウイ is pronounced *ui* and ウィ is pronounced *wi*
ウエ is pronounced *ue* and ウェ is pronounced *we*
ウオ is pronounced *uo* and ウォ is pronounced *wo*

The rule for the use of these variations is that ウ with little イ, エ, or オ is used for the names of people or countries. However, the rule is broken frequently, particularly in advertising. You will see examples of this in the せいかつ sections of your textbook.

D Draw a line from the name of each sport to its matching piece of equipment.

サッカー

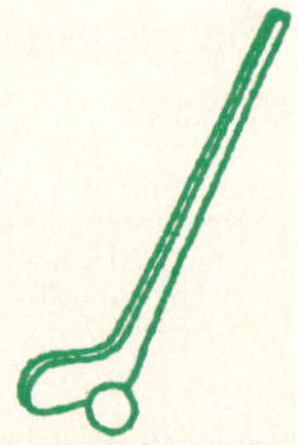

テニス

スキー

バレーボール

スクーバダイビング

ゴルフ

ローラースケート

ホッケー

E You are in the やきゅう team. Look at the baseball terms below.

ヒット	ホームラン	ピッチャー	バッター
オールスター	アウト	ストライク	ファースト

Which word would you be pleased to hear the umpire call? ______

Which word would you be unhappy to hear the umpire call? ______

F You are now able to write the names of all the きもの characters.

 なまえ

 なまえ

 なまえ

 なまえ

 なまえ

 なまえ

れんしゅう しましょう

A The names of many countries are written in カタカナ. Refer to the list of new カタカナ below and try to work out the names given on the map.

ウ	エ	ケ	サ	ソ	テ	ニ	ヌ	ネ	ノ	ム	ユ	ワ
		ゲ	ザ	ゾ	デ							

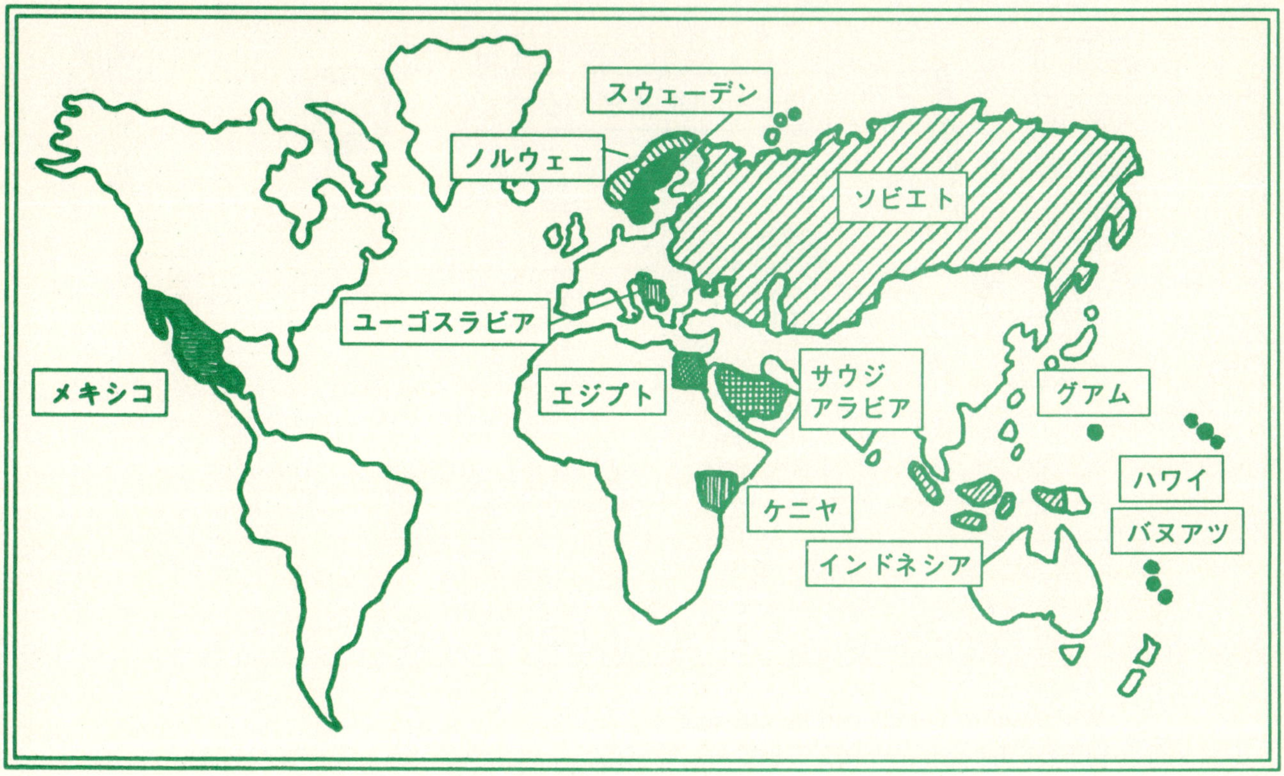

B Highlight which of the following you have at home.

ビデオ　エレベーター　テニス コート　バケツ

テレビ　フリーザ　ラジオ　シャワー　ピアノ　プール

C Highlight which of the following you have ridden on or in.

ケーブル カー　モノレール　カヌー　スノーモービル

スポーツ カー　タクシー　ヘリコプター　ジープ

オートバイ　スケート ボード　キャンピング カー

モーターボート

wa

ワ ワ ワ

ワ ワ

ne

ネ ネ ネ ネ ネ

ネ ネ

no

ノ ノ

ノ ノ

mu

ム ム ム

ム ム

yu

ユ ユ ユ

ユ ユ

so
ソ ソ ソ
ソ ソ

zo
ゾ

te
テ テ テ テ
テ テ

de
デ

ni
ニ ニ ニ
ニ ニ

nu
ヌ ヌ ヌ
ヌ ヌ

Set four

かきましょう

u

ウ ウ ウ ウ

ウ ウ

e

エ エ エ エ

エ エ

ke

ケ ケ ケ ケ

ケ ケ

ge

ゲ

sa

サ サ サ ザ

サ サ

za

ザ

G Label the items indicated in the illustration. The ローマじ spelling is given below.

kamera	retaa peepaa	herumetto	resutoran	
rajio	ootobai	gaarufurendo	booifurendo	teeburu

H Without referring to your previous practice, label the fruits and vegetables.

E There are many different flavours of ガム (*gamu*) available in Japan. Your friend has been given some and has asked you to translate the labels for him. In the space provided, write what each label is.

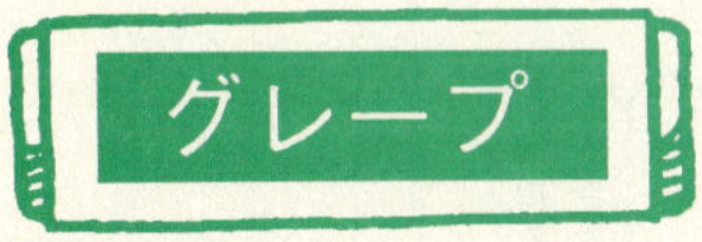

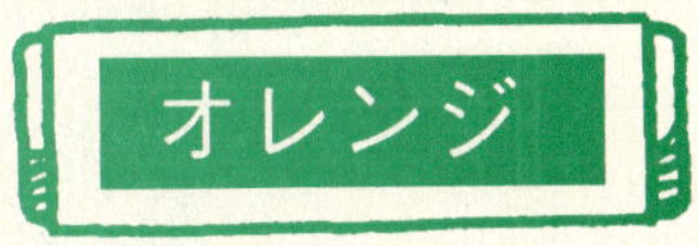

F Your friend パトリック is going to 日本 and wants you to label his family photo. パトリック doesn't do 日本語.

C Draw lines to match each カタカナ word with its English equivalent.

パセリ	jelly beans
レタス	orange
アプリコット	mango
セロリ	tomato
ゼリー ビーンズ	parsley
レモン	chicken
オレンジ	lemon
アボカド	lettuce
チキン	apricot
マンゴー	avocado
トマト	celery

D Someone has mixed up the animals' signs. Write the correct name for each animal on its sign.

れんしゅう しましょう

A The names of many fruits and vegetables are written in カタカナ.
To work out these names, refer to the list of new カタカナ below.

オ	キ	シ	セ	ハ	フ	ヘ	マ	メ	モ	ヤ	リ	ロ	ン
	ギ	ジ	ゼ	バ	ブ	ベ							
				パ	プ	ペ							

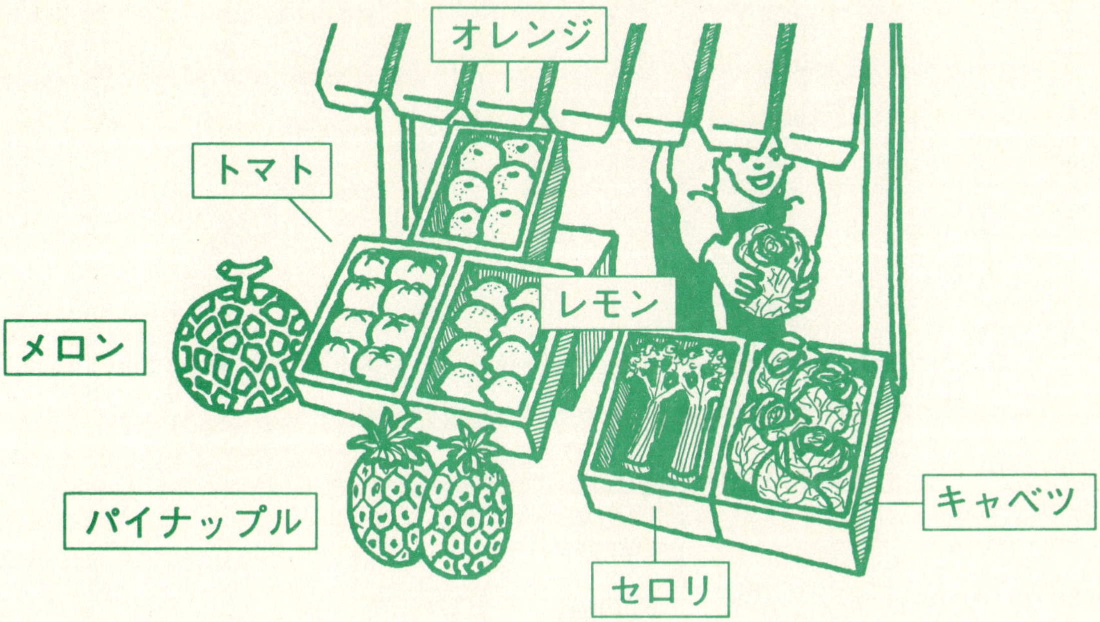

B Highlight the odd word out in each group.

1 スープ　マスク　バナナ　バター

2 カンガルー　ゴリラ　スカーフ　ライオン

3 スポーツ　ゴルフ　スキー　バレーボール

4 ヘリコプター　トラック　タクシー　ロボット

5 ポップス　クラシック　ロック　ギター

6 グレープ フルーツ　ハンバーガー　ハンカチ　マーマレード

ro

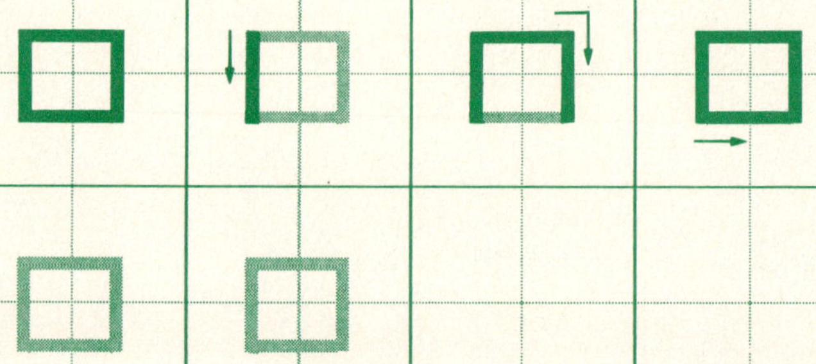

n

me

メ メ メ

メ メ

mo

モ モ モ モ

モ モ

ya

ヤ ヤ ヤ

ヤ ヤ

ri

リ リ リ

リ リ

ha ハ ハ ハ

ハ ハ

ba バ

pa パ

fu フ フ

フ フ

bu ブ

pu プ

he ヘ ヘ

ヘ ヘ

be ベ

pe ペ

ma マ マ マ

マ マ

Set three

かきましょう

o
オ オ オ オ
オ オ

ki
キ キ キ キ
キ キ

gi
ギ

shi
シ シ シ シ
シ シ

ji
ジ

se
セ セ セ
セ セ

ze
ゼ

G The class in the level below you can all say their names in 日本語 but can't yet write them in カタカナ. They have asked you to write them.

H Without looking at your previous practice, label these drawings of the drinks.

E ローマじ (roomaじ) has been given for these drinks and snacks. Rewrite the names in カタカナ.

koohii

hotto miruku

kokoa

chiizu

doonatsu

karee raisu

toosuto

tsuna

piinattsu

hotto doggu

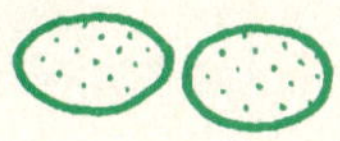
kurakkaa

F Practise writing the names for the drinks in カタカナ.

ミ	ル	ク

ア	イ	ス	コ	ー	ヒ	ー

ホ	ッ	ト	チ	ョ	コ	レ	ー	ト

コ	ー	ラ

C Label these items of clothing.

コート	トレーナー	スカート	スーツ

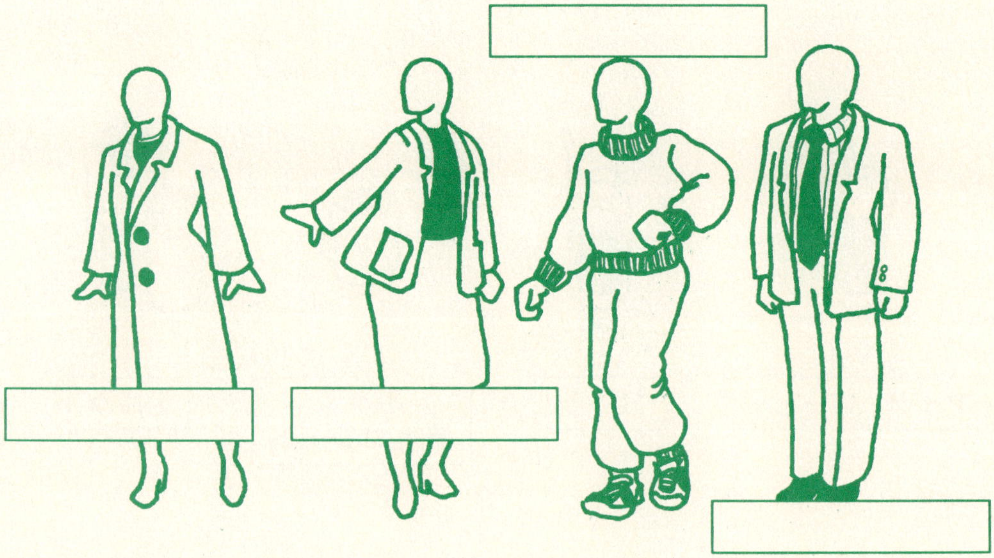

D Choose a word from the list below and write it next to its description.

トースター　カーヒーター　カークーラー　トラック　ポスト
スクーター　スコア　ココナツ　スピーカー　ポスター

1 used to mail a letter

2 decides who wins

3 used to make announcements

4 makes toast

5 used on a hot day when driving

6 looks good on a wall

7 transports people

8 used on a cold day when driving

9 transports goods

10 found in the tropics

れんしゅうしましょう

A Read aloud the names in カタカナ of the drinks below. Remember that little ツ is the カタカナ equivalent of little つ and that ー represents a double vowel.

アイス コーヒー　　コーラ　　ホット チョコレート　　ミルク

B Draw a line from each word to its matching picture.

コアラ

ボール

レコード

ヨット

トイレ

ドル

チョーク

ra

ラ ラ ラ

ラ ラ

ru

ル ル ル

ル ル

re

レ レ

レ レ

hi ヒ ヒ ヒ

ヒ ヒ　bi ビ　pi ピ

ho ホ ホ ホ ホ ホ

ホ ホ　bo ボ　po ポ

mi ミ ミ ミ ミ

ミ ミ

yo ヨ ヨ ヨ ヨ

ヨ ヨ

su ス ス ス
ス ス zu ズ

chi チ チ チ チ
チ チ

tsu ツ ツ ツ ツ
ツ ツ

to ト ト ト
ト ト do ド

かきましょう

a

アアア

アア

i

イイイ

イイ

ku

ククク

クク

gu グ

ko

コココ

ココ

go ゴ

れんしゅうしましょう

A Colour all stroke 1 lines red, all stroke 2 lines blue and all stroke 3 lines yellow.

カタカナ

B Practise writing カタカナ in both よこがき and たてがき.

C Complete these words, which begin with the new letters.

kamera  ＿メラ

gamu 

＿ム

takushii  ＿クシー

dansu  ＿ンス

naifu  ＿イフ

カタカナ

Set one

かきましょう

ka
カ カ カ
カ カ

ga
ガ

ta
タ タ タ タ
タ タ

da
ダ

na
ナ ナ ナ
ナ ナ